What a box of delights *The Little Book of Unexpected Poetry* is! Ruth Leigh's charm and wit are evident in spades, but so also is her compassion, her empathy and her understanding of the human condition. With a mixture of poem styles, genres and subjects, there's something for everyone here, and you will find yourself laughing and weeping in equal measure as you allow these words to both warm your soul and challenge you. A book to dip into, to savour and to love.

Liz Carter, author of *Repression Ground* and *Valuable*

THE LITTLE BOOK OF UNEXPECTED POETRY

Ruth Leigh

Resolute Books

ISBN 978-1-915981-24-0

Published by Resolute Books

Contents

Introduction 1

Life is Copy 3

Stars 5
There's No Nice Way To Say This 7
Thanks a Lot, Year 10 8
Language Barrier 12
An Unusual Blues Song 14
Making Gluten-Free Salad for Twenty-Eight 16
Poetry Ruined My Life 18
The Agony of the Writer 22

Recollected in Tranquillity 25

Doing Well 27
A Shot to the Heart 29
Apple Jelly 30
Danger Waits 32
The Imaginary Tiger 34
Don't Save 38
Some Suggestions 39
If You Are Not Completely Satisfied 41
Cousins 43

History: Just One Thing After Another 45

Sonnet 116.1 47
Gloucester Crescent 49
Vesuvius 52
Aunt Jane 54
Thank You Mr Rankin 57
Up In the Garret 59

The Other Ones 63

French Breakfast 65
Advice to a Teenage Girl 67
Dear George 68
X Marks the Spot, A Twitter Poem (written at 18.27 on 1st August 2023) 70
Paint Charts 72
Hashtags 74

The Unexpected Power of Poetry 79
Acknowledgements 85
Biography 86

INTRODUCTION

If you're surprised to be holding this book of poetry in your hands, it's nothing compared to the way I feel. You may know me as a writer of fiction, or a freelancer, or a speaker. Or you may not know me at all and have taken a punt on this slender volume. For which I thank you most sincerely.

I love poetry. When I was a child at primary school, I wrote an awful lot of it. Living as we did in a village in the middle of Epping Forest, I drew on nature very heavily for my early works and was often praised for my non-rhyming stanzas describing autumn leaves, willow trees, wildlife and so on. Then I went to high school and stopped writing it altogether. I still read it, but never thought I'd ever write another poem. But forty years on, I did.

In early 2023, I went to a spoken word event run by the wonderful Justine de Mierre. I read out one of my poems. People seemed to like it. I went again and once more shared my words. I was surprised to see the intent faces and tears being wiped away. In May this year, I began reading my work at Scripted Development at 1975 Wine Bar in Woodbridge. Each time I read my words out loud, I watched as people's eyes filled, as faces stilled, as the room seemed to gain an extra dimension. And then I thought, 'Maybe it's time to put all these poems together.'

I hope you enjoy them.

Life is Copy

I suppose you could call these poems miscellaneous. They come from real life events, observations, memories and snippets of half-heard conversations. They're fairly cheerful in tone, which is a good way to start a poetry collection I feel, and are written in a mix of styles, as you will see.

STARS

There we lay, twin souls, fingers entwined.
The scent of sweet grass in our hair,
the gentle zephyr at play.
We gazed, two lovers, at the sky full of stars.
Our hearts as one, our skin aglow.

'What beauteous sight is this?' quoth I.
As the firmament winked and gleamed above.
'Surely the stars themselves look down upon us
And weep for joy to see our love.'

Lo, I felt my lover's hand in mine, entwined
His eyes like twin stars gazing upon me
Gleaming starlight upon his countenance
His hair like liquid gold.

Said he, 'Why no, these stars upon which we gaze
Are no more than spheres of flaming gas
Whirling through space a million miles away.
They cannot think, or look, or weep.
For that is foolish and unscientific
and not based in fact.'

He added that the grass was damp
and the night air chilly
And that he had to get to work in the morning.
Mentally, I crossed stargazing off my list
of Things To Do
And wondered if ever I would find true love.

The idea for this poem has been lurking at the back of my mind for about 25 years. My husband, whom I met at sixth form, did his degree in chemistry and has a scientist's mind. I did mine in English Literature and have no idea how science or maths work. In spite of this, we get on very well, and he is my first reader every time I write a new book. He is most assuredly not the man in this poem, but I rather liked the idea of some flowery prose that then takes a completely different turn as the female half of the two star-cross'd lovers realises that this relationship is going nowhere.

THERE'S NO NICE WAY TO SAY THIS

There's no nice way to say this
Your poetry is poor
You keep submitting verse to us
It doesn't scan well and it's dour.

We've tried to be polite and kind
We answer every time.
But Marjorie, Submissions Ed
Is drowning in your rhyme.

She's not the perkiest of gals
Her menopause was frightful.
Hot flushes, whiskers, banging heart
Otherwise, delightful.

We know you love the Tartan Noir
Porridge, auld claes and murrder.
Well written, honest, we do too!
But please, take it no furrder!

I have absolutely no memory of writing this poem, but it must have been at some point after I joined the ACW (Association of Christian Writers) and discovered the term 'tartan noir' to describe the genre inhabited by such Hibernian greats as Ian Rankin, Val McDermid, Ann Cleeves and Wendy H Jones. I was surprised to find that it both rhymed and scanned and can only imagine I wrote it for a laugh, never thinking it would see the light of day.

THANKS A LOT, YEAR 10

Yeah, thanks a lot, all of you.
Lazy. Disorganised. Semi-feral.
That's what the head of year told me.
'Good luck!' he snarled, first day of term, teeth
clenched, eyes darting.
'Useless, the lot of them! Do your best
and see you on the other side.'

You're right. He is. A complete one of those.
A total and utter one. With bells on.
I was impressed by the drawing that accompanied
your comments on the tech toilet wall.
A few more adjectives wouldn't have hurt,
but in essence, you nailed it, Year 10.

Lazy? Don't think so. You work when you're
motivated. Who doesn't?
I'd like to see the head of year reaching his full
potential when he's being written off on a daily basis.
Disorganised? I lost your mid-term reports. Found
them again, but still.
There's a lot to remember and
you've all got a lot going on.
Semi-feral? Because you wear hoodies
and some of you have piercings? Get real!

Thanks a lot, Year 10. I locked my keys in the car
when I got to school on Thursday.
I was stressed out. I'd had another row with my
girlfriend, and my athlete's foot was playing up.
Not a good day.
''Sup, Sir?' you enquired politely, as you extinguished
your cigarette prior to entering a school building.
Ten seconds was all it took, and you were in. Fist
pump, big grin and our day began.

'Half-witted slackers, the lot of them.' More wisdom in
the staffroom from our esteemed head of year.
Who, I happen to know, has got a third in general
studies from the University of the North Circular.
Or something like that.
He is to teaching what Basil Fawlty is to hospitality,
Attila the Hun to diplomacy.
I may tell him so after my second pint at the staff
Christmas bash at the Turk's Head.

Thanks a lot, Year 10.
I've been questioning myself lately.
My girlfriend says it's not too late.
I could still make something of myself.
I was starting to agree, but that was
before I started teaching you.
Funny, disorganised, kind, lazy, loyal, semi-feral you.
I'm loving it. You're starting to get under my skin.

I saw you in Aldi last week, Ryan Cooke.
Big baggy coat, hands in pockets, head down.
I watched you slouching round the aisles
eyeing up the produce.

Hand on your shoulder.
Your mum on her crutches, asking for help
with the trolley.
No dad, three little ones and you.
Lazy? Uncaring? I don't think so. My eyes filled as I
watched your kindness unfold.

Thanks a lot, Year 10. You've taught me a thing or two.
Your eyes and minds are open wide, ready to take in
whatever's thrown at you.
I've deflected a few toxic pitches from our respected
head of year. Like you need any more crap.
I don't care about your untucked shirts and scruffy
hair. I can see past them. Unlike him.
Don't worry. I've got your backs.

Keep at it. Do your best. I can't ask for more than that.
Don't listen to the haters. You're better than them.
Try not to do drugs. I don't want to see you down the
underpass in five years' time.
You're the future. Not me.
Not our saintly head of year.
Remember that and grab all your opportunities with
both of your lazy, disorganised, semi-feral hands.

So, thanks a lot, Year 10.
You've changed my life. I hope I'm changing yours,
even just a little bit.
Two more terms and we say goodbye.
Keep at it. Chin up.
Respect.

I wrote this poem when my eldest son was in Year 10, in a rage that everyone had something narky to say about this age group. Everything was their fault, apparently – they were lazy, disorganised, disrespectful. The boys I drove to the cinema, hosted at sleepovers, and handed plates of pizza and garlic bread to at our house were none of those things. They were funny and kind and full of potential. I gave it the title as an ironic nod to the tone most people seemed to use about this year group. When I read it out for the first time, a young man came up to me, thanked me for speaking out and told me that the poem had touched him deeply. So, for all high school teachers and their students (especially the Year 10s), this is for you.

LANGUAGE BARRIER

What I want to say is this:
Your eyes are bluer than the bluest sky.
Your skin like molten caramel.
The sea whispers love as it laps the shore.

Your hand in mine is bliss. I want to love you and never stop.
I'm here but I won't be for long.
The sun beats down and warms my awakened heart,
The breeze's fingers play with my hair.

I'll miss the plane. I'll quit my job.
I'll learn your language and work at the hotel.
We were born to be together.
The sun slides slowly down the sky.

That's what I want to say.
What comes out is this:
'Yes, yes, is very good. Is hot, yes? I like.
I go England tomorrow on plane. Thank you. Bye-bye.'

This sounds like a love poem, but in fact was written in the intense heat of an Andalucian summer at my in-laws' flat. My mother-in-law is a fluent Spanish and French speaker and has taught languages all her life. When we visit the flat, we are the only people out of 21 families who are not Spanish, and English (quite rightly, in my opinion) is not widely spoken in the village. I would sit by the pool, or at a table in the humid afternoon with our neighbours, or in someone's flat, and listen to the rapid chatter, wishing most heartily that I could understand it. I speak pidgin Spanish, and to these warm, friendly people, my attempts must sound stilted and unnatural. But I do try, and putting my struggles into the mouth of a girl on her holidays longing to speak out her heart was the way this poem evolved.

AN UNUSUAL BLUES SONG

Woke up this morning, a doo be be doo.
I said I woke up this morning, a shoo be de doo
The rain was running down the windows
Looked like I'd be feeling blue.

I heard a noise, a doo be be doo.
Oh yes, I said I heard a noise, a shoo be de doo.
It was the sound of the kettle
My love was making a brew.

The month's too long, a doo be be doo.
I said the month's too long, a shoo be de doo.
By the end I'm brassic[1],
But who cares, coz I've got you.

Life is full of issues, there's so much to be done.
Housework and laundry, gotta do the school run.
Cooking and cleaning, it seems never ending
Texts and telephoning, emails to be sending.

The house is never tidy, I don't get time to tweet.
We're sometimes late for school, and the garden
isn't neat.

[1] Cockney rhyming slang. "Boracic and lint: skint."

There's stuff to sweat but hey, it's the end
of the middle eight.
I haven't got the blues coz
I'm married to my best mate.

I woke up this morning, oh shoo be doo be doo
Said I woke up this morning, a doo be doo be do.
My heart is full of love,
the children slept right through.
New day, sun's a shining, you lovely man, I love you.

Now this **is** *a love poem. I don't generally do rhyming verse, but if you're composing in the blues style, you have to have some kind of rhyming scheme. My husband and I love the blues and have a large collection on vinyl and have gone to see many bands in our time. This was written a while ago when the children were much younger, and these days the challenges are different. But nothing else has really changed – still got weeds in the garden, still running to keep up, still married to a lovely man. Shoo be doo be doo.*

MAKING GLUTEN-FREE SALAD FOR TWENTY-EIGHT

No one else will, they said
And you know how it goes
We've got hundreds to feed
And at least twenty-eight chose

The gluten-free option
We can't let them down
So I'm stuck in my kitchen
And I think I might drown

In gluten-free pasta
Red onions and salad
I might as well use it
To compose a new ballad

All life is copy
That's what I believe
The words won't stop coming
There is no reprieve

What is it with Christians
And fellowship lunches?
Acres of quiche and
Mixed leaves in bunches?

Someone must make it
And it seems that it's me
The vegans are next
Then it's dairy-free

Thank heavens for Joy
The lady who bakes
I can boil up fusilli
But I say no to cakes

She's in her kitchen
Surrounded by icing
While I chop up peppers
And fret about spicing

Lord bless this salad
Both with gluten and without
Next year it's a no
I'm not cooking nowt.

I was in the midst of putting this book together when I had a Zoom call with the Priceless Ladies, five fellow writers. The Ladies support each other through good times and bad, offer advice, shore up dented confidence and are just the kind of gals you want by your side. One of them appeared on screen apologising for the fact that she was wielding a large spoon and wearing an apron. 'I'm making gluten-free pasta salad for twenty-eight,' she announced, a line that simply begged to be used in some literary form. I don't think there is any hidden meaning. It's just a poem about making an awful lot of gluten-free pasta salad.

POETRY RUINED MY LIFE

It did. Everything was fine.
Working five days a week, went to the gym, had a life.
Beers with the boys, footie on a Saturday.
Netflix and chill with my girlfriend.

She does great presents. Every time.
Season tickets, vouchers, things I love.
Then this one day, she says, 'Want a surprise?'
And raises her eyebrows in that way she's got.

She takes my hand and off we go, up to the bedroom.
I can guess what she's got in mind.
You've got to love a surprise.
I do.

She puts her hands over my eyes, whispers, 'Ready?'
I can hear rustling.
I won't lie. I'm excited. It is my birthday.
Gotta be a special treat.

Eyes open and it's like Christmas morning! What's it going to be?
I rip open the paper… it's a book. A book with writing and no pictures.

Hang on.
Hang on just a sec.

She's smiling into my eyes and squeezing my hand, so
I say,
'Wow. It's amazing. Thank you!'
We kiss.
She nestles into my chest.

Turns out she read something in one of her
magazines.
Getting closer to your man's feminine side.
I mean I like females as much as the next man.
But reading? Do me a favour.

'It's poetry, darlin',' she says, kissing my ear.
'Loads of it, not like what we did at school.
Modern stuff. I tried a bit and I like it.
I thought we could read it together.'

Well, you can't be rude, can you?
I mean, I love her and all that. She's the nuts.
So, I smile and kiss her back and say I love it.
Then she gives me my other present.

That's a bit more like it. We're knackered after
so we just chill.
I forget all about the poems. Life goes on.
One day she says to me, 'Read those poems yet?'
And I have to come clean.

What's the worst that could happen?
I mean, they're just words.
It's not going to kill me. So off I go.

I'll read one and call it a day.
Some bird with three names wrote it. I skim the words
and then it happens.
I'm hooked. It's about this bloke with a knife killing
his pets[2].

It's sick. I love it. I want more.
So, I read and read and read till my eyes are blurry
and I need a beer.

So, there it is. I'm not the man I used to be.
I read poems. I even wrote one the other day. My
girlfriend loved it.
I mean she really loved it if you know what I mean.
She says real men aren't scared of their emotions. She
thinks it's hot.

Poetry ruined my life. Tell you why.
I love it. I do. It's cool but I can't tell anyone.
It's my dirty little secret.
My friends would laugh their heads off and call me a
dick.

So now I lead a double life. Beer, footy, work, the gym.
One of the lads.
At home, rhyming couplets and stanzas and stuff.
Who'd have thought it?
It's true, poetry ruined my life.

---

[2] If you're a poetry fan, you might recognise this reference to Carol Ann Duffy's magnificent and chilling poem, 'Education for Leisure', removed from the GCSE syllabus in 2008 by AQA, who seemed to be missing the point.

The idea of a man's man who likes his beer and football and has never really explored his feminine side having to conceal his new-found love for verse made me chuckle, and this poem pretty much wrote itself. I liked the notion of a dirty little secret not being some kind of 21st century vice but a carefully hidden addiction to the written word.

THE AGONY OF THE WRITER

Upon Waiting for the Muse to Alight (circa 1822)

Come, thrice-blessed muse and alight
Upon the mind of she who writes both day and night.
Lo! As the rosy-finger'd dawn doth paint the sky
And birds sing sweetly at the break of day
Let thy beauteous form appear
To one who waits for inspiration to strike.

The Tyranny of the Blank Page (circa 2022)

Today I must complete at least
Two articles and cook the tea.
My fiction goes from famine to feast
My readers wait for number three.

Facebook can wait. I shall not scroll.
My tax return is overdue.
Ooh! A DM! How very droll
Cup of tea? Go on! Get you.

I'll just do Wordle. Good for the mind
And check my Insta – only for five.
It's nearly twelve, tired of the grind
I'll make some lunch – gotta stay alive.

Where is the muse? Whence has she fled?
Is that a new follower on TikTok?
So tired – 'tis nearly time for bed.

In common with most of us who earn a crust by our pens, I probably spend far too much time procrastinating and scrolling, hence this verse. You'll notice that by the final stanza, the weary poet has given up with scansion and uniformity. As she would.

Recollected in Tranquillity

Lots of people have said lots of things about poetry over the years. I frequently quote the Bard of the Lakes, William Wordsworth: 'Poetry is emotion recollected in tranquillity.' And so it may well be. Having already felt all the emotions, my poetry doesn't make me cry. I read 'Doing Well' at Scripted Development, and I was surprised to see a young woman wiping away tears, which were pouring from her eyes. I had obviously touched her in some way with my words. I'm not a massive fan of crying, but if what Wordsworth said is true, then other people's emotion can arouse strong feelings.

DOING WELL

Thank you, yes, we're all doing well.
The children are fine. Work is good.
Thanks for asking, we appreciate it.
We're all doing just fine.

We're doing well in the sense that we are all still alive.
No-one's bleeding. No-one's crying secretly
in their room.
As far as we know. We haven't lost the plot.
We're soldiering on, fighting the good fight.

Glance sideways at us – don't we look good?
We smile, we laugh.
It's not as if a bomb, detonated two generations ago
Has shaken us to our very foundations,
Leaving us teetering on shaky ground.

It's not as though the shock waves of explosions,
Hanging in the sky like toxic fireworks
Have shaken the roof, battered the windows
And shattered the structure of our life. We're fine.

You've seen those pictures taken during the War,
Haven't you? Houses with their fronts
and sides sliced off.
Carpets and curtains and furniture in situ,
Laid bare, exposed, shivering while everyone stares.

We're not like that. We're all doing well, thank you so
much for asking.
If we keep on smiling and telling ourselves we're fine,
Then maybe the house will right itself, the
foundations stop shaking,
And next time you ask us how we are, our answer will
not be a lie.

Without revealing that I had authored it, I set a writing exercise to an adult group to compare 'Doing Well' with Brian Bilston's 'NHS Test Results'. I was interested to hear what everyone had to say. They picked up on the war imagery through the poem, which hadn't occurred to me at all as I wrote it. The two poems both address fairly desperate situations, one familial, one corporate. If you have a pencil about your person, feel free to scribble on the poem and find a copy of 'NHS Test Results'. Money spent on any of Brian Bilston's collections is a real investment.

A SHOT TO THE HEART

Years ago, you injected me, with a shot to the heart.
It cut off all feeling, made me numb.
I should thank you.
But I can't.

That pinprick's been multiplied a thousand times,
A million pins piercing a million skins.
I can't stand the pain.
Thank you.

Sometimes, the shortest poems are the most powerful. Two stanzas were enough to express what I was feeling when I wrote this one.

APPLE JELLY

I remember that day so well. September, apples rosy on the trees.
Leaves just starting to turn. The smell of woodsmoke in the air.
I popped round for coffee, as I so often did then.
And there you were, making apple jelly.

The sharp smell of fruit in the air, the sound of bubbling from the stove.
Quick cutting with your sharp knife, pips and stalks and leaves intact.
You flung open the cupboard door to reveal treasure within.
Jar after jar of clear gleaming apple jelly, chilli-jewelled and glowing.

'It's easy. You should try it,' you said, smiling as I held the muslin bag for you,
Apple pulp dripping luxuriously into the waiting silver bowl.
'No peeling or coring, just cut them up and chuck them in. Boil vigorously.'
We both laughed, liking the idea of a really good vigorous boil.

You had less than three autumns left. Neither of us knew that day.
If we had, my tears would have dropped into the apples and ruined the set.

My sobs would have drowned out the sound of
laughter, the scent of coffee.
You were still well, your years uncounted and no end
date in sight.

Like that sharp knife quartering the fruit, your days
were numbered.
Like the sugar boiling with the fruit, our memories
were sweet.
Like the glorious autumn colours, it was all over
too soon.
Too soon.

Since then, every year I harvest the apples and forage
for fruit.
I line up the chutneys and jams and fruit jellies.
I gaze into the bubbling, fragrant, vigorous boiling
and see you as you were.
Smiling in your kitchen, generous, kind, loving till the
last.

This poem was written about my friend Judith. When she died, the pain was almost unbearable. It was about four years later that I wrote this poem, when the sharp agony of loss had abated to a dull ache that never really went away. I didn't have to make anything up. This is exactly what happened. Even now, I see a pair of earrings or a scarf in a shop and think to myself, 'That would be the perfect Christmas present for Judith' before I remember that I will never put a hand-written card or a gift into her hands again. This poem wasn't exactly emotion recollected in tranquillity, but I think the four years between her death and me writing it were needed.

DANGER WAITS

Like a bear, fuddled from long sleep, confused and heavy eyed
He lumbers from the door, waiting to be told what to do and where to go.
The growls and heavy paws not to be given credence
The need for sweetness, for balance of his ragged moods is all he craves.

Much more dangerous and to be avoided at all costs is the snake
Waiting smiling by the door with arms outstretched.
Will she strike or stroke? Uplift or send you hurtling down into the depths?
Such a long and weary climb back up. So long. Oh so weary.

This house is a dangerous place for children. They should not, must not go there.
Those imprisoned inside press pale and desperate faces against the glass.
'Help us,' they whisper, but the smiles carefully flickering on their faces,
The sweet tones, the compliant nature (unnaturally constructed from long experience)
Keep all offers of assistance away, arms stiff and outstretched.

A blow from the bear's paw leaves a bruise, but the skin is rarely broken.
The venom from the snake drills deep into the soft arms of the children,
Hands raised to protect themselves from the anger, voices low and eyes cast down.
Poison driven far into the tender veins, waiting to catch them unawares.

In that final winter, the bear is tired, his shaggy head bowed, grateful for love.
The snake uncurled, her scales dull and uncared for, her fangs blunted.
The children show their scars to each other, whisper confidences, stumble on understanding.
The danger is past, the future hopeful, the way clear to joy, long awaited.

I remember a conversation I had some years ago with someone who had been part of a group of people who oversaw the welfare of vulnerable children. His view on them was not necessarily the same as that of his colleagues. He would listen to a report and ask the same question: 'Who's looking out for the child?' The words of tenderness and compassion he used about little children touched something in my heart, and the words began to flow.

THE IMAGINARY TIGER

Meet Stripey. He's my oldest friend.
The imaginary tiger.
He came to live with me
The day my mum stopped loving me
And all the cuddles ended.

Look at his fur. It feels like sunshine.
I snuggle him and he feels so soft.
His eyes are kind and he never bites.
I know he loves me.
I just know it.

Stripey comes with me to school every day.
My imaginary tiger.
Without him I'd be lost for sure.
He sits under my table and lies on my feet.
He never shouts out or gets told off.

I get so sad. I get so cross.
I can't help it.
Mum says I should never have been born.
Then other times she laughs too loud
and squeezes me.
People stare. I hate it.

I've got two real friends.
Three if you count my imaginary tiger.
They are kind and listen to me when I shout and cry.
Afterwards they pat my arm and smile.
It heals my heart.

Sometimes I think I am going to burst.
I shout and throw things and the grownups get cross.
They give me stickers if I'm good.
I hate stupid stickers.
It's so unfair.

Stripey says one day we'll run away together.
At night I lie in bed, and when I've stopped crying,
I build a house in my head.
A house to live in with no shouting or banging.
Huge fields to run in, flowers that don't die,
friends next door.
I can't wait.

My friends know about Stripey even though
they can't see him.
No one else does. Not my mum.
She would laugh and say things in her
sharp, glittery voice.
I've tried to love her, but it's hard.
Loving my tiger is easy.

Last week we went to the zoo.
Our class and the one above.
Stripey came on the coach with me, obviously.
We sat on the back seat.

There were lions and seals and penguins and snakes
and a shop at the zoo.
And tigers.

I felt weird about going to see the other tigers.
I did though. I had to. They make you do stuff when
you're a child.
They had scary eyes and big claws and huge teeth.
Not like Stripey.
We chatted about it at bedtime.

Stripey hasn't got claws. He says claws are
no good for cuddling.
His eyes are kind and look at me like
he is glad I was born.
I never think about his teeth, really. They're just teeth.
We snuggled up and drifted off to sleep.
Me and my imaginary tiger.

I've got to go and live with my granny in another
place far, far away.
I've got to leave my school.
My two real friends cried when I told them and
hugged me.
I wanted to cry, but the tears are stuck in my heart.
They won't come out.

There was so much shouting at my house.
I hid in my room with Stripey.
A man came, and a lady, to help me say bye-bye to
Mum and start my new life.
I'm scared. Now I know. No one loves me.
Except my imaginary tiger.

This is one of the saddest poems I've ever written, and it came about when my daughter came home from primary school and told me about the imaginary tiger. The phrase really resonated with me, and as I learned more about the little boy who owned Stripey (because to him, he was real), I felt the words of this poem fighting to get out of my brain. Very sadly, the little boy was taken from his mother and sent to live miles away. He was terribly upset about leaving my daughter and her friend. They were all so little – no more than eight – and I hated to think of what life had in store for him. I feel such anger for children like him who don't experience love and support at home and cannot access the help they need because of cuts and misguided government policies. Sometimes poetry is about trying to change the world. I wish there was no need for imaginary tigers, but sadly, our world is full of them.

DON'T SAVE

In fact, cancel.
That's probably what you should do.
Saving is hard, and it wears you out
Especially when people don't want to be

Don't save is a good option
But then you have to stand by
Watching as it all falls apart
Tears, pain, loss, anger

Cancel. The third option
Just do that
Don't bother
Not today

When I wrote this, I was still trying to fix people. I've stopped now. The title came to me as I was writing something on my laptop and it gave me options. Around the same time, I realised that I too had options and that I was tired of being manipulated by people who enjoy creating unnecessary drama.

SOME SUGGESTIONS

In retrospect, you should have got a dog.
Loyal, obedient and easily trained to do your will.
I've never heard of one answering back or forming
its own opinions.
A dog. That's one suggestion.

Looking back, maybe a goldfish would have
done the trick.
Gazing out at the world, trapped, happy to do the
same thing day after day.
No need for emotional interaction or empathy.
A goldfish. There's another suggestion.

With the benefit of hindsight, a canary might
have suited you.
Living in a cage with no possibility of flying free.
Wings clipped, beak blunt, gazing at itself
in a mirror all day.
A canary. Now that would have been a plan.

Having thought it through, perhaps a cat
would have worked well.
Aloof, self-possessed and haughty.

None of those inconvenient emotions, tears
or joy to stress you.
A cat. What a super idea.

In fact, really, having had my whole life to consider
these suggestions,
Anything, fish, fowl or mammal would have been
better than what you actually did.
Thank you so much. Years of misery and reproach and
for what?
You should have got a dog.

Parenting is hard, and no one gives you a manual. You would hope that everyone does the very best they can with what they're given, but this is not always the case.

IF YOU ARE NOT COMPLETELY SATISFIED

If you are not completely satisfied, please let us know.
We will endeavour to rectify any mistakes or
imperfections in our product.
To the best of our abilities, it leaves us in excellent
condition
Although its journey to the final destination may
cause some damage.

Although the journey to the final destination has
clearly caused considerable damage
We cannot be held responsible as our terms and
conditions clearly state.
Sadness and no longer playing the game cannot be
attributed to us.
We apologise for any inconvenience. Sorry.

To the best of our abilities, it left us in perfect
condition.
We cannot be held accountable for its
incomprehensible behaviour of late.
This is not what it was manufactured to do. Factory
settings can be applied.
We are sorry that you are not satisfied. Terms and
conditions apply.

Embarking on any life change is a dangerous business. If you are truly committed to it, people will start to say, 'You've changed!' and they don't mean it in a good way. You will begin to realise that the world is full of people who look like adults but who behave like children. You will speak less and listen more. I'm fairly sure that this poem is about someone who has stopped playing games and is starting to realise that this will limit their social circle considerably.

COUSINS

And there we stand, the three of us, in the sunlit garden.
Summer nineteen seventy. Green grass underfoot, sunbeams streaming,
The scorching heat on our bare arms and legs.
Standing. Smiling. Gazing. Scowling.

Already, even then, I'm not happy. My face set, a pout, a clenched fist.
You two smiling, gazing, arms around me, standing close.
Thank you. Even then, even then, on my side.
Standing. Holding. Keeping. Loving.

Fifty years on we stand, the three of us, outside the room.
Spring twenty nineteen. Smooth floor underfoot, raindrops falling,
The chill of loss on our bodies, heavy.
Standing. Crying. Hugging. Loving.

Now, I'm better, certainly on the way. My face soft, not ashamed of tears.
You two sobbing, hugging, arms around me, standing close.
Thank you. Always, ever since then, on my side.
Cousins. Trusted. Valued. Loved.

I wrote this poem when I unearthed an old black and white snap of me standing in a back garden. My two cousins are with me. I am in a pink dress with daisies embroidered on the yoke (I can see it now). My dark hair is cut short in a bob. I must be three years old, rising four. My cousin, who must be around eight, stands behind me with her arms around me, smiling into the sunshine at whoever is taking the photo. Her younger brother, six, stands next to me, eyes screwed up, fists on hips, ready to dash off the minute the photograph is taken. My sister is not yet born, but her arrival is imminent. Four years ago, the three of us converged on a hospice in Lincolnshire. Their mother, my aunt, much-loved, had little time to live and we came together again to say goodbye. I will never forget sitting on her bed, holding her hand and gazing into her eyes. I could see the love in hers and the warm, practical, supportive affection that came from this branch of the family is one of the best and most uncomplicated things in my life. Again, although my sister is not able to be there, her presence is. She is miles away, using her remarkable caring skills to look after the elderly and vulnerable in a way that I never could. Just because someone is not in a photo (or indeed a poem) does not mean they are not there.

History: Just One Thing After Another

As an eighteenth and nineteenth century nerd, writing poetry about people and civilisations long gone was always going to happen. With the benefit of hindsight, the savvy poet can pick up on fragments of family gossip in letters, the footnotes in classical works and anomalies in the biographies of well-known Great Writers to produce a new, yet familiar work. I wrote the poem about Catherine Hogarth (Mrs Charles Dickens) quite some time ago. Catherine's features and personality always seemed to be hidden in the shadows, and I thought it was time she had a poem all to herself. Having recently published a collection of short stories around minor characters in Pride and Prejudice, I have only just put the tottering pile of biography, scholarly exposition and fan fiction back on my bookshelves, and Miss Austen, the favourite aunt of many of her numerous nieces and nephews, was not yet quite ready to join them. The others were inspired by such disparate events as my mother-in-law's wedding, a visit to Pompeii, an attention-grabbing headline in 2019 and a brief trawl through some Lyrical and Romantic Poets' works.

SONNET 116.1

Let me not to the marriage of true minds
admit impediment.
Or at the very least, let me not say what
I actually think.
God forbid.
Imagine how that might be.

Love is not love which alters when it alteration finds.
You could call it love,
But it's something else altogether.
Something much nastier and more secret.

It is the star to every wandering bark.
In other words, a cloud which hangs, waiting,
o'er all it sees.
Ready to descend,
To play its game unchallenged.

Love's not Time's fool.
Oh no. Too wary and too practised for
anything like that.
A light which blinds, a beam which smarts,
Leaving the earth scorched, mangled in its wake.

Even to the edge of doom it goes, boldly.
Proudly even.
That sickle bending to the tender flesh,
the vulnerable soul.
The damage done, the slate wiped clean.
Scratched and broken on that ever-fixed mark.

If this be error, and upon me proved
Then never did I live, nor see you moved.

I am a big fan of parody, done well. I do love a sonnet and some years ago, I came across this one and amended it for my own ends to reflect a coercive relationship. I hope Shakespeare doesn't mind. I read out a completely different sonnet by the Bard on the occasion of my mother-in-law's wedding to a lovely man. They were 91 and 84 when they got married, living proof that there is hope for us all.

GLOUCESTER CRESCENT

If I'd known then what I know now,
The ringlets fallen out of curl, the sparkle all but gone,
The bombazine in place of floating muslin—
I would have said no when you asked me.

If I'd known then what soon became plain,
Your dear Mouse, darling Tatie, my own dearest
darling Pig,
Become a slow and docile drag on your brilliance—
Never would I have gone to your birthday Ball.

If I'd known then what pain you'd give me,
My nineteen-year-old self would have
looked elsewhere.
Kept my heart to bestow on one who truly loved me,
Who would not drive a dagger into my soul.

Ah yes, if I'd known then what I know now,
The jokes and puns and wordplay gone sour,
Your eyes darting to my sister – the Judas!
I would never have accepted your turquoise ring.

If I'd known then what anguish you would inflict,
Killing Dora and marrying Agnes,
I'd have pretended to be asleep many more times
than I did—
I can tell you!

If I'd known then what all the world now sees,
My love o'ershadowed with a crushing dread,
My darlings' love usurped and my seat at
the table taken—
I would have stayed a spinster.

And yet, husband, still I love you.
That young and passionate man who loved me once,
Who swept me up and carried me off—
Breaking my heart and shaming me to the world.

And here I sit, old, fat, nearly forgotten,
Entombed in this silent Crescent.
My own dear boy my champion yet—
Not many left, but a few to treasure.

But yes, had I known then what I know now,
You could have married that simpering Beadnell girl
for all I care.
And left me Miss Hogarth, happy, light-footed,
content—
Instead of poor, abandoned, shadowy Mrs Dickens.

When I was a child, I would often sit in my special secret place behind the big armchair reading a book from my parents' bookcase. I was far too young, at eight years old, to understand David Copperfield, *bound in blue and gold and with no pictures. Still, I read it again and again, devouring the description of David's birth, his idyllic early life with his mother and Peggotty, shuddering at the dark shadow that fell over The Rookery when the Murdstones arrived, and feeling emotion stir in me at young David's passionate love for Dora. I read pretty much all of Dickens in my adult life and accepted without question the standard introduction written by his friend Forster. In this, his wife Catherine was described as 'a slow, shadowy kind of person who never really suited him'. The cruelty and injustice of these words didn't really strike me until my thirties when I began to read around Dickens and came across Claire Tomalin's book,* The Invisible Woman. *Dickens fell in love for the second time after his disastrous courtship of Maria Beadnell (the inspiration both for Dora Spenlow in* David Copperfield *and, less kindly, Flora Finching in* Little Dorrit.*) The object of his affection was Catherine Hogarth, the eldest of George Hogarth's 10 children. She was 19 when she met her future husband, who invited her to his 23rd birthday party. They married and embarked on a career of writing (him) and childbearing (her). Catherine bore 10 children and lost two, suffering through a succession of painful births and crippling post-natal depression. Her younger sister Georgina Hogarth soon became the housekeeper in the Dickens household, taking over many of the duties of Dickens' wife. In the summer of 1858 they separated, and Catherine moved into a house in Gloucester Crescent. I thought it was about time Catherine had her own voice.*

VESUVIUS

October. A warm evening as I gaze across the bay.
Late sunlight striking sparks of pure fire from the sea.
Our house near finished and our lives together
beginning.
How I love you, my dear one! How precious you are!

I write to tell you that I stand near our house.
Marcus the builder scribbling with charcoal
on the walls.
Do not worry, my treasure, my angel.
He writes only to assure himself of the position
of the beam.

Unseasonal weather. I almost fancy I feel the full
summer's heat on my cheek.
The smell of woodsmoke in the air.
I confess that I tremble as I stand here, the earth
beneath my feet not quite solid.
Our dreams, our hopes made real here before me.

How long have we waited, you and me? How long?
Your father unsure of my prospects, my mother in
need of my care.
But now, one week only from our wedding and our
house almost finished.
Surely the gods smile upon us, bless our union, this
perfect autumn day.

My darling, my own, my heart is yours. Our lives
forged together like links in a chain.
My heart as full of passion and love as the volcano
that winks at me across the bay.
Our future as rosy as the red and orange sky
over Naples.
Our marriage fruitful as the slopes down to the sea.

I send this now, with my love and a kiss for your
beautiful face.
My own one, seven days and the house will be ours.
Pompeii, where we will live out our days, raise our
children, be joyful.
Its streets and buildings the backdrop to our love.

Be happy, my dear one, and know I am near.
I sail late this evening.
Believe me that nothing can stop me.

Twenty years ago, my husband and I got 99p flights from Stansted to Ancona in Italy for a long weekend. It was cold, and there weren't many people around, perhaps one of the reasons for the extreme cheapness of the flight. We visited Pompeii and Herculaneum and drove up Vesuvius. Like every visitor, we were stunned by the immediacy of the ruins. People just like us had lived, worked and loved here and had their futures stolen away from them in a cloud of fire and ash. As we shivered in our freezing cold hostel room, wrapped in blankets and sipping thin hot chocolate made with not quite boiling water, I gazed across the Bay of Naples at the silent volcano and wondered what that must have felt like. This is my take on the disaster, couched in the loving words of a soon-to-be husband to his soon-to-be wife, which adds to the poignancy of the whole thing.

AUNT JANE

She does not come often enough to visit us.
So say I to Mama, who scolds me.
'She is often here, Fanny, and you are an ungrateful girl
To say otherwise.'

I love Aunt Jane. I do not tell Mama how much, but I do.
She laughs like a girl although she does not dress like one.
Always a cap and a serviceable mended gown
Not like Mama's rustling silks and beaded slippers.

The two aunts are often looked for
And when the carriage is sighted, we run down the drive to welcome them
Me and Edward and Henry
And the little ones far behind.

Mama narrows her eyes and creases her brow as she stands in the hall
Although her lips speak welcome her face does not.
Why does she not love Aunt Jane as I do?
Why does she purse her lips when speaking out her name?

Can not she see the wit and the life in her eyes?
Does not she share my joy in the company of one who weaves such tales?
Almost another sister, my aunt once whispered.
More like a beloved friend than one of many neices[3].

Once, hiding behind Father's chair in the library
I hear the aunts whispering, their voices like mice in the wainscot.
'Jealous.' 'Affection.' 'Bitter.' 'Breeding.' 'Worn out.'
I know not of whom they speak, but their words are filled with secrets.

The aunts sit quietly in the parlour.
One sews for my new brother or sister, one writes.
Aunt Jane tells me stories and reads my tales
And tells me to write, always, Fanny, never give up.

One day I shall marry a handsome prince, I say
He will take me away to a faraway land
Where I will live in a palace
And my hair will turn to spun gold like a princess.

Aunt Jane laughs and strokes my cheek.
'Ah, dreams, child! Of love and golden hair.'
Her skirts rustle as the hidden paper whispers quietly
Caught between her dress and the chair where only she may sit.

Her stories are her children, she tells me
Destined never to be known or read widely.
She must write. She must or lose her reason.
She smiles her secret smile and looks away.

---

[3] Not a spelling mistake. This is how it was spelt in Austen's time.

Mama is upstairs awaiting the new baby.
'Eleven!' scolds Aunt Jane to her sister.
'What can Edward be thinking? She will be worn out.'
I hear the fear in her voice.

I think that eleven children are no worse than ten.
The noise and the crying and the nursemaids—
It is well that we are rich.
It is well that Mama never ails.

Aunt Jane has written me a new tale
All for my very own.
'To Fanny,' it says, in her impatient handwriting.
'From her own beloved Aunt Jane.'
I shall show it to Mama as soon as she is recovered.

This poem is written in the voice of Fanny Knight, later Lady Knatchbull. She was one of Jane Austen's favourite nieces, the eldest of 11 children born to Edward Austen Knight and his wife. The couple had 11 children in 16 years, Elizabeth dying of her last confinement when her eldest daughter was 15. Jane and her sister Cassandra often visited the Knights at their home in Chawton, Hampshire. Their brother had been adopted by wealthy, childless relations, hence his surname and economic comfort. In the nineteenth century, now a respectable Victorian matron, Fanny wrote disparagingly of her aunt and the Austens in general, earning her the dislike of Janeites all over the world. In her youth, however, she adored her Aunt Jane, a feeling that was reciprocated in full measure. I liked the idea of a teenage girl in a house of many brothers and sisters waiting at the window of her splendid home for two spinster aunts in worn clothing to come up the drive.

THANK YOU MR RANKIN

'Crime novelist Ian Rankin has gifted his literary archive to the National Library of Scotland in Edinburgh.' Headline from 23rd May 2019.

Thank you, Mr Rankin. What a gift. Your archive.
Gosh.
We don't know what to say. All those notes
about murder.
We're blown away. Thank you.
Honestly. We are. On behalf of the nation,
we're grateful.

Fifty boxes. Goodness. That's over twenty one feet
Of shelving. We had to get some new ones.
And sacrifice the kitchenette. We buy our coffee
in now, Mr R.
But it's worth it to have the Godfather of
Tartan Noir's archive right here.

We've had other offers, we won't lie.
None as good as yours. We'd love to hear from JK.
Maybe your letters will spur her on. No rush.
Rebus.

My archive is nothing compared with yours.
Dust and ashes.
No letters from fellow authors. Some reviews.
Lots of ideas.
A letter saying I was the love of his life (I wasn't).
An overdue tax bill. Some articles in the Parish News.

It seems extremely unlikely that anyone will want me
At any point to gift my literary archive to anyone.
But I shall continue trying to be the kind of writer
That the National Library of Scotland might like.

And this poem, although it has a body count of zero
Is at least a good place to start.

The pedantic reader (and is there any better kind?) may be questioning whether this poem belongs in this section. I read this headline on 23rd May 2019, and I put it to you that that is aeons ago. This was pre-Covid society. Words and phrases such as 'lockdown', 'self-shielding', 'being pinged by the app', 'social distancing' and 'doomscrolling' were yet to take over our lives. A fresh-faced Ian Rankin spent many hours in the National Library researching novelist Muriel Spark for his PhD and wrote several of his novels in its august surroundings. If that doesn't qualify this poem to sit comfortably alongside Jane Austen and Shakespeare, I don't know what does.

UP IN THE GARRET

There is a perfectly good drawing room, warmed by a crackling fire.
My room, the bed heaped up with wraps and furs
Would be the ideal place to write.
But no.
I am a poet, and therefore to the garret[4] I must go.

We poets have heads full of fragments of news and words and rhymes.
Did you know, dear reader (for I must address you thus as up in the roof I shiver)
That the word 'garret' comes from the French
for watchtower?
No?
Non?
I thought not.

Downstairs, where my sisters and Mama sit sewing
There are clusters of beeswax candles making night into day.
The maid has banked up the fire against the raging storm outside.

---

4 For some reason, poets seem to belong in a draughty garret with only a guttering candle and a diminishing supply of ink for company. It's just another word for attic and seems to have become shorthand for what struggling writers must go through.

Up here in my garret the draughts sigh
around my feet
My tallow candle gutters and my pen spatters ink.

I wear my embroidered writing robe.
I must, in truth, else the muse will flee and
desert my poor pen.
We poets are a race apart.
Comfort and warmth inspire us not.
Our words crowd in upon us while hunger
gnaws our bellies
And the creditors bang upon the door.

Not that any such folk would dare to intrude
upon Mama
The respectable widow of a Baronet and
mother of five.
But there is no need to mention this, dear reader,
if you would be so kind.
A garret is the natural place for a spinner of tales
A maker of rhymes
Even if he does have a good income and belongs to
two clubs in St James'.

A trope, I think they call it.
Volumes of poetry must be slender.
Dawn is never anything but rosy finger'd.
The muse will never light upon the wealthy living in
comfort.
And we poets belong up in the garret.

I first came across the word 'garret' when reading Little Women. *Jo March, the literary tomboy of the four sisters, spends a good deal of time in hers, writing furiously for money to support her family. As a freelance writer, I've often made jokes about not being able to wait for the muse to descend upon me as a client is waiting for six hundred inspirational words about radio programmes/a house for sale/some flowers by next Tuesday. The idea of someone fulfilling those expectations while living a comfortable life in the non-poetry part of their existence tickled me, and hence this poem was written.*

The Other Ones

Having never written a book of poetry before, I didn't realise that you could have a miscellaneous section. The other poems fell fairly obviously into headings and, for the sake of clarity and completeness, I decided to ~~lump together what was left over~~ carefully place these last odes in their very own special constituent part. Some are a bit cross, some a bit sad and some even have elements of humour and romance.

FRENCH BREAKFAST

Long, languorous breakfast, emerald water crashing
over slippery rocks.
The scent of good coffee, contented murmuring.
Crumbs of glistening croissants lasciviously dropping
to the floor, unheeded.
Crisp linen (white), salty tang, those towering waves.

And afterwards, on the beach with you,
our hands entwined,
We watch the foaming tide rush towards us,
eagerly, greedily.
A million shells and grains swept out to sea with the
boom of surf
Unthinking, violent, beautiful.

Who named them French Breakfast? We laugh to
think of those peppery globes
Crunched up and swallowed with café au lait,
every day.
But only in Paris. Or Aix-en-Provence. Peut-être.
A beret tilted rakishly over one eye.

The names we call things. How funny. How sad.
We call this love and soon it will be dividing,
a million times
Like oysters, like bivalves, like the shimmering
rock pool.
New horizons.

French Breakfast. Not a meal, but a place, a memory,
a refuge.
Whenever radishes are mentioned (and that's not
often)
We'll smile and laugh secretly to ourselves
Remembering that morning in Brittany. Waves
towering.

This poem springs from happy memories. My favourite place on earth is Brittany. There is something about its rocky coast, emerald seas and rock-strewn beaches that soothes and inspires me as nowhere else can. My husband and I visited it many times before our children came along, and I suspect that the memory embedded in this one is me sitting at a table at a restaurant in Cancale in the April sunshine, pregnant with our first child who finally showed up in late August. My husband had tried growing French Breakfast radishes in our Essex garden, and the name made me laugh and sparked this poem.

ADVICE TO A TEENAGE GIRL

The world is a better place because you are in it
You don't have to do what he tells you
Especially if his suggestions come with a side
of guilt and shame.
Go out with your friends. A lot.

Listen to the music that makes you happy.
See your friends.
You really don't have to do things you feel
coerced into doing.
Honestly. Talk to your friends.

Love is not about limiting your horizons
They're meant to be widened.
Drink water. Get some fresh air. Go out
with your friends.
And don't do what he tells you to do.

If you've got this far, you can probably work out where this poem is coming from.

DEAR GEORGE

Thank you for your letter of the fourteenth instant
Without prejudice
Without compassion
Without understanding

George, I thought we had a deal
But all that cash you've been rolling in
Seems to have caused some kind of hearing
impairment

You see, George, out here in the real world
The little people have to work to make a living
Every day
Like, with not enough sleep and trying to achieve a
work-life balance.

Like, with family and bills to pay and
everyday worries.
So when Niagara came to our town
And I had to break out the umbrellas and
launch a canoe
I was a little upset.

I'll be honest with you, George,
More than a little.
I don't mind shopping and cleaning and staffing
and marketing
And doing my tax return and VAT and income tax

And working out menus and chatting to customers
And designing the interior and the menus
And sorting out my website
And thinking of new ways to make a living

I really don't.
But I do mind water pouring down my walls.
And I'm not crazy about it dripping through the lights
And endangering my staff.

Dear George.
It's not hard.
I pay.
You do the right thing.

OK?

I was very cross when I wrote this poem. I'm not a fan of people with lots of money who think they are above the law. If I should ever become enormously rich (and at the time of writing, it doesn't look all that likely), I would not move house, buy a fancy car, or start hobnobbing with people with over-filled bank accounts. I would use my new-found wealth to make people's lives better. Those who lie and cheat and are strangers to morals deserve to have poems like this written about them.

X MARKS THE SPOT, A TWITTER POEM (WRITTEN AT 18.27 ON 1ST AUGUST 2023)

Scrumptious sardines!
About to go full Turtle Mutant
Writers, how do you feel about using swear words in your book?
Some typos have real consequences.

Have you ever doubted your decision to become a writer?
The local news station used my rain picture.
One objective of Proverbs?
I finally have a Kindle.

Guess where I was today?
Remind you of anyone?
Yay! Thanks for tagging me in, Chloe.
Happy release day.

A quick hello and good morning.
Could you spend a month here to escape from the world awhile?
Do you have any MCs with a kill count of zero?
Do you like reading historical fiction?
Bambi and I have arrived at Hayfield.

I've got something very exciting to show you all tomorrow.
One minute you're a shy teenager.
OK, I don't get all the fuss of the bird changing to the X[5].

"Scrumptious!" he said to my chest as I put his plate down.
What? You ate him raw?
If it's warm, would you walk barefoot outside?
When reality breaks in your palms, all you're left with is an all-grey mess.

Crikey – my book's only gone and made it to the shortlist!
And book #14 has left the building.
Pythagoras, very good at math, dead now.
What do you need in your writing space to stay focused?

This is simply the first line of all the tweets on my feed at 18.27 on Tuesday 1st August 2023.

[5] I would beg to differ here, fellow Twitter user. I hate the X. But it did give me a great idea for a poem.

PAINT CHARTS

May, a soft and bloomy day in Springtime.
On the fells we wandered, you and I, in drifts of Heath and Lavender
We'd planned it out, back home in London Soot
Plotting on maps, with Silver Compass and Neon Highlighter.

Climbing up into the Wild Blue Yonder, you took my hand and said,
'I love you.' Thank you. I never thought anyone would.
'You are my Supernova. Bright White, White Cotton, Starburst, Snakeskin Superstar,' you said.
I didn't mention the unseen breath of the elephant in the room.

You said you love me, so it must be true.
I know I Reciprocate, but how to say it?
Love was not encouraged nor modelled in childhood
These feelings are new, but Delightful,
Sandstone Scary.

May, a soft and bloomy day in Springtime.
On the fells we wandered.
Before returning to our Home Sweet Home
Redbrick Joy and Elements of Pea in the London Soot.

Since becoming a freelance writer, I have developed a number of low-key superpowers. For example, I can detect a certain brand of designer paint and the exact shade 99% of the time, just from photos. I appreciate that being able to fly or become invisible at will would probably be more useful in everyday life. However, as a long-term freelance writer, these qualities have stood me in good stead. Whoever is in charge of naming the paint at the said company deserves not one but many medals. Eagle-eyed readers will spot the references to some of their products. I rather like the idea of decorating the pantry in Reciprocate, the drawing room in London Soot and the small summer parlour in Sandstone Scary. I shall await the call...

HASHTAGS

You need to stop. I've been silent for so long.
I told myself I could deal with it.
No one else thinks it's weird.
Or annoying.
Just me.

So please, I'm asking nicely.
Stop it. I don't like it.
Every day something different.
It started with cats. Cute cats. Falling off things.
Randomly.
I thought, 'OK, that's your thing. I respect that.'

But now I'm fed up. Stop it please.
The cats turned into memes. Annoying cutesy memes.
I hate them. I could smash something. But I won't.
I'm too nice.

And now it's your life. Your perfect, lovely life. Every darn day.
A walk on the beach. Pancakes for breakfast. A just because treat.
Proud mum alert statuses.

Honestly. You need to stop now. I'm asking nicely.
I feel rage rising in me like a tide.
A tide of crashing, angry, foaming water breaking on a shingled beach.
Here it comes. It will only take one more thing. Or maybe two.
Depends.

A hashtag would do it. #makingmemories. #andthenthishappened.
Filters are for coffee. And vacuum cleaners. Not your picture-perfect photo life.
We all know. We all know your husband drinks and you've never had enough love.
We know that. And we're sorry.
I'm sorry.

But just the same. I'm going to say it one more time, and then I don't know what I'll do.

Please don't do that. I don't like it.

This was my first poem. It sprang from the early days of Facebook, when everyone was busy engaging in the new fun activity of pretending that everything in their lives was absolutely marvellous. A working mother of three children with no family nearby to help out, I would read statuses about perfect family walks, home-made breakfasts and wonderful holidays and wonder what was wrong with me. How come all these other busy mums could balance their work and personal lives so effortlessly? What was I doing wrong? This sorry state of affairs continued until one morning at the toddler group when another mum put me straight: 'You don't actually believe all that stuff, do you, Ruth?' she said, smiling incredulously.

I felt very slightly better, although I continued to compare myself to everyone on social media and come off worse for some years to come. As this was the first poem I ever wrote, it seems right to end the collection with it. If I was a proper poet, I would have talked more about rhyming schemes and villanelles and quatrains and suchlike. In spite of the sad lack of such elements, I do hope that you have enjoyed it.

THE UNEXPECTED POWER OF POETRY

When I've finished reading a book, I generally look up information on the author via the power of the internet. You can do that if you would like to, but I thought I'd make it easier for you by putting it all down on the page.

So here's some background on why I think poetry is a powerful and life-changing medium.

I became a full-time writer in January 2021. I had a fairly healthy freelance portfolio and had just brought out my first novel. The minute I took the leap, my biggest freelance customer stopped sending me work. Undaunted, I carried on, writing my second novel and then my third and continuing with the freelancing. However, it soon became clear that I would need to find other streams of writing income. I attend events at the weekends where I sell my books directly to the public. I go into high schools and give inspirational workshops.

I love all my work. But walking into a high school and facing a great many teenage people, many of whom have absolutely no interest in English, or, indeed, actively loathe it, is my very favourite thing to do. I've often wondered why it is that going into a situation where most of my audience are not in the least interested in what I am going to speak about is so much fun. Often, the teacher takes me at my word when I ask them to give me the students who really hate my subject, and I am confronted by a roomful of young people with their arms folded and their eyes narrowed. 'What fresh hell is this?' they seem to be thinking, as they gaze at the enthusiastic middle-aged woman in front of them. 'As if being forced to read Shakespeare and contrast and compare stupid poems isn't bad enough.'

This attitude is meat and drink to me as an inspirational speaker. I start by telling them that I won't be talking at them. It will be an interactive session. I can almost hear their thoughts: 'Yeah, yeah. Whatever.' They glance at their phones, only to find that time is dragging, as it will when a person is trapped in a classroom learning about something they have no interest in.

We carry on, and I surprise them by revealing that I had a terrible time at school and hated it more than I can tell them. Several pairs of arms unfold. I then tell them that I was always being told off for staring out of the window, daydreaming and listening to other people's conversations. Eyes start to focus. Now, I assure them, those three traits are vital weapons in my armoury as a writer.

I segue smoothly into my first anecdote. It's summer 2021, and the second lockdown has just lifted. We are off on a family holiday, but the NHS app pings me to say I have to stay at home for 10 days as I've been exposed to someone with Covid. The rest of the family pile into the van and drive north while I stay at home and write furiously. In due course, I board a plane and sit in my seat, clutching my never-fail Aeroplane Book[6] to take my mind off what is to come. As I scan the familiar pages, I become aware that four or five seats ahead of me to my left, a row is going on. The two people engaged in said row are speaking at just the right volume for

---

[6] The Victorian House by Judith Flanders. I am such a nerd. Reading a book about the way our nineteenth century forebears lived, replete with footnotes, takes my mind off the fact that I am trapped in a metal tube hurtling through the skies.

an eager writer/eavesdropper to hear every word. They are a middle-aged woman and a boy of around 13. The conversation goes something like this:

Mum: 'No. I've told you again and again. You are not having an iPhone 12.'

Boy: 'It's so unfair! Everyone at school's got one.'

Mum: 'I don't care. Your father and I have told you. You're not having it.'

Boy: 'You're so lame!'

Mum: 'I don't care. The answer is still no.'

There is a slight pause. The boy is thinking hard. He comes out with his killer line: 'Aiden's got an iPhone 12.'

The mother shoots him a look of complicity, which he returns. Their body language changes completely. Both sit up straight and raise their eyebrows. She speaks, her voice heavy with coded meaning. 'And we all know why that is, don't we?'

At this point the plane takes off, and I never do find out what Aiden did to get his phone. No one except the mother, her son and presumably Aiden's friends and family will ever know.

By now, nearly all my listeners have unfolded their arms and are looking interested.

I give them their first task, which is to spend the next five minutes telling me why Aiden got the iPhone 12. I don't care about spelling, grammar or handwriting. They have free rein.

And off they go, even the most reluctant amongst them, scribbling away frantically and producing a clutch of gripping stories. It never fails.

'OK, Ruth, that's all very well, but what does it have to do with poetry?' you may well be asking at this point.

Stick with me.

Duly softened up, the students cannot wait to hear their words read out loud by me. One enterprising young scribe sent Aiden to the zoo where he fell into the orangutan enclosure and was squished. He was in hospital for months, and the large insurance payout funded his new phone. Others have him blackmailing his best friend's father who is having an affair. Sometimes he's part of a drug dealing family, or robs houses, or sets up his own business and becomes a millionaire. Some of the more acute students slip street language and mildly naughty words into their stories, betting on the fact that the respectable looking middle-aged woman in their midst will not understand the words and will certainly not read them out loud in front of their teacher, for goodness' sake!

She does. None of the eyes are narrowed by now.

The final piece in the jigsaw comes halfway through the workshop where I ask them what they think about poetry. My all-time favourite moment in a session came when I was teaching 320 restless Year 7s at a local high school. I mentioned that we would be looking at poetry, and a little boy in the front row clapped his hands theatrically to his head, leant forward and cried, 'Oh no!' in tones of utter horror.

So why I am telling you this? Because in every case, sharing poetry and talking about it softens up even the most obdurate of high school students. OK, I do read out a poem which none of them expect ('An Unusual Cat-Poem' by Wendy Cope), but still, it's not the subject you'd expect to engage Year

7s to 9s. I still don't quite understand why this should be, but my recent experiences with the awesome power of the spoken word has led me to realise that this is a subject that needs a lot more daylight shone upon it.

I often talk to the Year 7s about poetry and ask them what they think it's all about. I tell them I'll read them my favourite poem and declaim all 21 words (title included). There is a stunned silence every time, then they start to laugh. After we've analysed the poem a little bit and talked about the cat (they get very worried about whether it's a real cat and what it died from), I read them the first few stanzas from Thomas Gray's 'Elegy Written in a Country Churchyard'. Because 'An Unusual Cat-Poem' is, of course, mock-elegiac. Everyone then breathes a sigh of relief that they don't have to plough through such a long complex poem and we carry on with a touch of Brian Bilston.

When I teach adult creative writing workshops, poetry also hits the spot. We do a bit of contrasting and comparing, analyse poetic language and talk about how the words affect us. It's a powerful medium, and whether I'm talking to teenagers or middle aged ladies, it strikes me that it has the potential to change the world.

So, poetry is unexpected sometimes, but therein lies its power.

ACKNOWLEDGEMENTS

I very much doubt that any of these poems would have been written had it not been for Ken Ashton. I owe him a great debt of gratitude. Thank you to my first reader, my husband, who manfully ploughed through these poems although he is more used to critiquing fiction; to my colleagues at Resolute Books for giving me the opportunity to publish them; and to Clare, Raph, Sarah, Tania, Sue and Pete, Fortune, Justine and everyone who has ever listened to me and said, 'That gave me goosebumps.'

BIOGRAPHY

Ruth is a novelist and freelance writer, the author of the *Isabella M Smugge* series, contemporary humorous page-turners, and *A Great Deal of Ingenuity*, a collection of short stories about minor Pride and Prejudice characters. She lives in rural Suffolk with three children, one husband and a cat. You can find her on Instagram, Facebook, TikTok and Twitter at ruthleighwrites and at her website, ruthleighwrites.co.uk.

Printed in Great Britain
by Amazon

51084444R00056